DEC 13

For civil rights activists the
world over —J. P. L.

Library of Congress Cataloging-in-Publication Data
Lewis, J. Patrick.
When thunder comes : poems for civil rights leaders / by J. Patrick
Lewis, 2011–2013 Children's Poet Laureate ; illustrated by Jim Burke,
R. Gregory Christie, Tonya Engel, John Parra, and Meilo So.
p. cm.
ISBN 978-1-4521-0119-4
1. Children's poetry, American. 2. Civil rights—Juvenile literature.
I. Christie, R. Gregory, 1971–ill. II. Title.
PS3562.E9465W38 2012
811'.54—dc23
2011045938

Book design by Lauren Michelle Smith.
Typeset in Felina Serif.
The illustrations in this book were rendered in oil, acrylic,
and watercolor.

Manufactured in China.

10 9 8 7 6 5 4 3 2 1

Chronicle Books LLC
680 Second Street, San Francisco, California 94107

www.chroniclekids.com

when THUNDER comes

Poems for Civil Rights Leaders

BY J. PATRICK LEWIS
2011–2013 Children's Poet Laureate

ILLUSTRATED BY JIM BURKE, R. GREGORY CHRISTIE, TONYA ENGEL, JOHN PARRA, AND MEILO SO

chronicle books·san francisco

The poor and dispossessed take up the drums

For civil rights—freedoms to think and speak,

Petition, pray, and vote. When thunder comes,

The civil righteous are finished being meek.

Why Sylvia Mendez bet against long odds,

How Harvey Milk turned hatred on its head,

Why Helen Zia railed against tin gods,

How Freedom Summer's soldiers faced the dread

Are tales of thunder that I hope to tell

From my thin bag of verse for you to hear

In miniature, like ringing a small bell,

And know a million bells can drown out fear.

For history was mute witness when such crimes

Discolored and discredited our times.

the activist

We wept when the man was taken,
But we knew it was meant to be.
Daylilies drooped in the garden;
Night birds fell dumb in the tree.
We expected the worst of the future,
For the future was seldom bright,
And they carried away on the killing day
The last of the first daylight.

She moved to the front unbeaten,
Stepped slowly up to the board.
When she lost the man to the Ku Klux Klan
Her silent shadow roared.
Out in the enemy country,
Death marshaled itself for a fight,
But she led a choir in the line of fire
The first of the next daylight.

Stand tall, stand all my children,
Put away the sinister guns.
Embrace the boys that Hate employs,
Like mothers do their sons.
Daylilies can bloom in the garden,
Night birds can sing in the night,
When dignity has set us free
The rest of the best daylight.

Coretta Scott King
Civil rights leader
1927–2006

the
Auntie

When the people called me Daw, meaning
Auntie or Madam, the General hiccupped.
When my husband, who was not allowed
to visit me in Burma, died of cancer,
the General took a holiday.

When I was awarded the Rafto, Sakharov,
Nehru Prizes, the Congressional Gold Medal,
the General brushed the dust from his epaulets.
When I won the Nobel Peace Prize for defending
the rights of my people, they changed Generals.

When I refused food to protest my detention,
the new General stuffed himself on mangoes
and banana pudding.

When a cyclone flicked off the roof of my prison
like the Queen of Hearts, turning my life to shame
and candle, the General had a mole removed.

When they added four words to the constitution—
my name—to bar me from ever running for office,
the General signed it with his fingernail made of
diamonds and disgust.

Aung San Suu Kyi
Burmese pro-democracy activist
1945–

THE
SLUGGER

Our national pastime by the name
Of baseball was once mired in shame.
A prejudice-sized fear
Whitewashed the truth when history wrote
An unforgivable footnote—
The asterisk career.

Tape-measuring his home-run success,
800 of 'em more or less,
Won't get you very far.
Josh Gibson always knew the score . . .
Only to die three months before
The black man broke the bar.

He hit a mile the Jim Crow snub—
"No coloreds in a white man's club."
All anyone could do
Was name him to the Hall of Fame,
A tower in the tarnished game
That Gibson never knew.

Josh Gibson
Baseball Hall of Famer
1911–1947

Mamie Carthan Till
Mother
1921–2003

the innocent

Dark on that Mississippi Delta day,
My baby Emmett fell so far from grace
That Justice . . . what would Justice have to say?

I taught him not to sass or disobey.
They said he shamed a white girl to her face.
Dark on a Mississippi Delta day,

They beat him bloody, oh, they made him pay.
They kicked him, shot, then drowned him just in case—
And Justice could not find the words to say.

The killers were acquitted, by the way,
As Southern virtue gussied up in lace
Dark on a Mississippi Delta day.

They closed Emmett's casket to my dismay.
Seemed like to me it was a hiding place.
So Emmett's mama found the words to say.

I laid my bloodied boy out on display.
But fifty thousand mourners won't erase
Dark from that Mississippi Delta day
When Justice did not have one word to say.

THE VOICE OF
THE VOICELESS

The outcast sits and prays, or sleeps,
Untroubled by a human's touch.
From his oppressive seat, he keeps
Away from you at least as much.

His house is on the street: the curb.
His body signifies, Beware.
The flag he waves, Do Not Disturb,
No one can see, and still it's there.

Such savage rites, decreed by caste,
Divined by birth, and quick with rot,
Ensure one hostage to the past
Will be this godforsaken lot.

My children, I shall end my days
Reminding you: Your greatest sin
Done to these humble castaways
Is to forget the state you're in.

For we are not the ones to say
What will erode and what endure,
Where the iron, where the clay,
Who the foul and who the pure.

Mohandas Karamchand Gandhi
Political and spiritual leader of India
1869–1948

the captive

I was a typist, nothing more.
I loved my life, I hated war.

But it was war that stole from me
My job, my life, serenity.

They put me in a hateful house—
Internment camp—and I, a mouse,

Refused to squeak like most of these
One hundred thousand Japanese,

Until the day I told the man
What constant thoughts my heart began:

I am a typist, nothing more.
And I am no conspirator!

For 18 months, they tired the sun
With talking. In the end, I won

The freedom to resume all three:
My job, my life, serenity.

Mitsuye Endo
Japanese American interned during WWII
1920–2006

FREEDOM SUMMER

That day in June we stopped in Meridian, I reached in my pocket for the penny I called Hope. The Negro barber nodded, Y'all come back soon. In Longdale the KKK had burned down Mount Zion Church. We had left the inferno when Sheriff Price ordered us into a cruiser for a shortcut to county jail. With the odor of pee running down my pant leg, Mickey whispered, Don't expect that one phone call, and he was right. They fed us potatoes, peas, poke salad, and spoon bread. Our last supper. But once the Klan ambush was set up, the sheriff fined me $20, and told us, Git gone for good. Then the whole thin shimmer of our lives evaporated like smoke in a fog. Armed with cone-hat conviction and long-necked persuaders, the Klan rode in for last rites to the first rights of a gaunt trio. Flames licked the car as it sank under Bogue Chitto Swamp. After single shots to the heart had taken Mickey and Andrew, they'd saved three bullets for me. Freedom Summer is Forlorn Winter at the tag end of living. And just before they pitched our bodies into earthen graves on Old Jolly Farm, I remember that my hand was in my pocket. I could still feel Hope.

James Chaney, 1943–1964
Andrew Goodman, 1943–1964
Michael Schwerner, 1939–1964
Civil rights workers in Mississippi

the journalist

I am a woman with a foreign face—
Apple-pie American (born Chinese).
Nothing I do will ever hide my race.
Nothing I am bears those parentheses.

I wield a pen, this fine and fearless sword,
To open doors for which there are no keys.
The written word's the law, the law's the word.
No one I know deserves parentheses.

The newspaper I work for is the place
I bring these hate-crime villains to their knees—
Writing the wrongs that plague the human race.
Nothing I am wears those parentheses.

Whenever foreign faces take the stand
Against injustice, fear deadens their pleas.
Nothing I am, except a helping hand.
Nothing we are, chained by parentheses.

That foreign face, my countryman, is you,
Whose ancestors once settled overseas.
Congratulations, you are foreign too,
Though seldom have you worn parentheses.

Helen Zia
Chinese American activist
and journalist
1952–

THE ASTRONAUT

You should have seen the Onizuka bird,
The wingless aviator who would spend
Countless hours aloft, and afterward,
No longer have to say it's just pretend.

He soared around the Earth as in his dreams,
Then tried to stride the stratosphere again.
The world saw sudden grief in ragged streams
Where, for a little while, joy had been.

To honor him, they called an asteroid
Onizuka. Likewise, a dark dune
Now bears his name: across a rocky void,
An 18-mile crater on the moon.

Ellison Onizuka
Japanese American astronaut
1946–1986

THE LONG WALKER

My name means "in the center of the ground."
(Ojibwa—Nowa Cumig). Long ago,
My path was charted for me. I am bound
To lead our people and to strike a blow
That treaties be enforced on sovereign land
And our traditional cultures be preserved.
Invincible and proud, we make our stand
Till Native American interests are served.
We long-walk with the Hualapai, Diné,
Apache, and Yokuts to demonstrate

A universal principle: We say
We are of earth. Before it is too late,
Let's walk so softly on the hemisphere
Not even birds will know that we were here.

Dennis James Banks
Cofounder of the American Indian Movement (AIM)
and Anishinabe political activist
1937–

THE CRUSADER

I knew my rights meant nothing.
I kept them out of sight.
Seen and heard when the sun went down,
hidden in harsh daylight.

Then Liberation called one day
and asked would I consent
to tell the world that I was proud
of being different.

I took the fight to the city fathers.
They scolded me for that:
*We don't approve of boys who wear
an unconventional hat.*

So I became a city father
to break the laws that kept
boys and girls from living lives
that Life would not accept.

They say I came before my time
but who else would redress
unmitigated suffering due
to such small-mindedness?

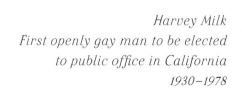

Harvey Milk
First openly gay man to be elected
to public office in California
1930–1978

banker to the poor

Start small, he thought. And so he did.
In Jobra, 42 poor women shyly
strike the first bargain. They will make
bamboo chairs for the $27 he takes
from his wallet.

Encourage them, he decided.
An impoverished gatherer of silkworm
eggs marvels at the miracle in her hand:
her community's very first cell phone—
now common in over 100,000 villages.

Empower them, he agreed.
A beggar joins ten other beggars
around a pond to catch eel and carp—
and profits. Money lures dream fish.

Promise them, he thought, a future.
Contagion of pride, hope ascending,
a young girl telling her school friend,
We will soon be eating sweet rasgulla,
kalojam, and cham cham. Just you wait.

Muhammad Yunus
Bangladeshi banker
1940–

the statesman

It is as if he's landed on the moon
Five years before the actual event.
At Robben Island Prison, his descent
Into a nightmare world, an outcast dune,
Begins at forty-six. His fate derails.
There are no clocks, his life's defined by bell
And whistle, sisal mats (no beds), his cell
Is seven feet square. But destiny prevails.

He keeps for an eternity of years
His keepers, not the other way around,
Marked by a calm refinement so profound
As to alleviate his captors' fears.
He said, once they had turned the jailhouse key,
No man will rob me of my dignity.

Nelson Mandela
Former President of South Africa
1918–

THE FIRST

I run down
the line, eight feet,
nine . . . and feint to feel
the rush between the third
baseman's brush back and home.
Whitey Ford stares through me, a sneak thief
playing on his disbelief, a phantom blackbird hopping
on and off

the dare, flinching,
inching along the ledge
to legend. I time the windup,
my pistons primed to shovel under
Yogi's glove. Yankee Stadium is stunned!
But you can hear the cheering all the way from Harlem.

Jackie Robinson
First African American baseball player
in the modern era
1919–1972

 the child

Sylvia pushed into the wind,
Septembering the trees,
and hurdled over a railroad track
to a two-room shack
that never read "Browns Only."
It did not have to.

Under the billion-acre sky,
she wondered, *Did white girls
at 17th Street Elementary really
wear rainbow necklaces?*

Aunt Sally took her there once.
Eyes sharp as icepicks pierced
the windowpanes as if seeing
a Mexican for the first time.
Every door was locked with a
secret combination of frowns.

How can anyone ever get in?
Sylvia asked. *Someone must know
who has the right key . . .*

She looked up at her mother.
Maybe me?

*Sylvia Mendez
Mexican–Puerto Rican–
American civil rights leader
1936–*

the activist

Coretta Scott King: During Dr. Martin Luther King Jr.'s extraordinary career, his wife, Coretta, spent most of her time raising their four children. But even then she alternated mothering with civil rights movement work by speaking and organizing church, civic, and peace groups. After Dr. King's death, she came into her own. She met with many of the world's great spiritual and political leaders and became heavily involved in preserving her husband's dream of peace and equality through the Atlanta-based King Center for Nonviolent Social Change. *Resource: http://www.thekingcenter.org/csk/bio.html.*

the auntie

Aung San Suu Kyi: Burma (now Myanmar) achieved independence from Britain in 1948. But the end of colonialism did not mean freedom. Military strong-arm tactics were used to deny Burma's citizens basic freedoms, repress dissidents, and exile hundreds of thousands of minorities. A staunch pro-democracy advocate and nonviolent reformer, Aung San is often referred to as Dr. Suu Kyi to distinguish her from her father, Aung San, the founder of modern Burma. She holds a Ph.D. from the University of London. Despite repeated protests from foreign governments, human rights organizations, the Pope, and the Dalai Lama, she has spent a total of fifteen years under house arrest. In 2007 she was put on trial for harboring, for two days, an American man who swam to her lakeside home. Sentenced to three years of hard labor (suspended), her freedom was negotiated by American diplomats. Later released from house arrest, Suu Kyi met with the military head of Myanmar on August 19, 2011, and said she was "satisfied" with the outcome of those talks. *Resource: Wintle, Justin.* Perfect Hostage: A Life of Aung San Suu Kyi, Burma's Prisoner of Conscience. *New York: Skyhorse Publishing, 2007.*

the slugger

Josh Gibson: Josh Gibson is a legend wrapped in a myth surrounded by a mystery. He died at the young age of thirty-five and never made it to the white major leagues, but in his career, he hit "almost 800 home runs," according to his posthumously awarded plaque in baseball's Hall of Fame. The stories about him run up to the edge of belief and sometimes beyond. "I played with Willie Mays and against Hank Aaron," Hall of Famer Monte Irvin once said. "They were tremendous players, but they were no Josh Gibson." Jackie Robinson received credit deservedly for being the first black American to play in the major leagues. But Josh Gibson, though little-known today, would surely have been the first had it not been for the rampant racism that engulfed America at the time of his prominence. *Resource: http://sfgate.com/cgi-bin/article .cgi?f=/ c/a/2006/05/05/SPGQNIL8UR1.DTL.*

the innocent

Mamie Carthan Till: When fourteen-year-old Emmett Till made a trip from his home in Chicago's south side to visit relatives in Money, Mississippi in 1955, he had no idea what awaited him. He and his friends stopped to buy candy at Bryant's grocery store. Accounts differ as to what happened next. Emmett either said, "Bye, baby," or whistled at the store owner's white daughter—a "crime" evidently punishable by death in the Deep South. His executioners beat him, shot him, and left his body in the river to swell. They were acquitted by a white male jury in 67 minutes. Emmett's mother insisted that her son's body be shown in an open casket as a symbol of Southern brutality. Thousands attended Emmett's funeral in Chicago. *Resource: http://afroamhis tory.about.com/od/emmetttill/a/emmetttill.htm.*

the voice of the voiceless

Mohandas Karamchand Gandhi: Perhaps more than any other person, Gandhi—the father of India and the Mahatma ("Great Soul," an honorific title)—pioneered resistance to tyranny through nonviolent civil disobedience. Throughout his life, he worked to ease poverty, broaden women's rights, and build religious and ethnic harmony. He also fought to promote the rights of "untouchables," the desperately poor, have-not segment of society, shamed by India's higher castes. Gandhi ate simple vegetarian food and fasted for long periods for self-purification and social protest. He lived to see his country's long struggle for independence from Britain realized in 1947. After several unsuccessful attempts on his life by others, Gandhi, while on his nightly walk, was shot and killed in New Delhi in January 1948 by a radical Hindu. *Resource: Brown, Judith M.* Gandhi: Prisoner of Hope. *New Haven, CT: Yale University Press, 1989.*

the captive

Mitsuye Endo: In the wake of Japan's December 7, 1941, attack on Pearl Harbor, many West Coast Japanese nationals and second-generation Japanese Americans, known as *Nisei*, which means "second generation," were forcibly moved to "War Relocation Camps." A handful of Japanese protested the outrageous denial of their civil rights. Mitsuye Endo lost her job as a clerk in Sacramento's Department of Motor Vehicles and was sent to camps in California and Utah. In *Ex parte Endo*, 323 U.S. 283 (1944), the U.S. Supreme Court found, on December 18, 1944, that the internment was an "unconstitutional resort to racism" against loyal citizens like Endo, and therefore thousands upon thousands of other prisoners. In 1998, Congress passed legislation that apologized for the U.S. internment of Japanese people and paid each surviving internee $20,000, which totaled $1.2 billion in reparations. *Resource: Ng, Wendy L.* American Internment During World War II. *Westport, CT: Greenwood, 2002.*

freedom summer

James Chaney, Andrew Goodman, and Michael Schwerner: In the early 1960s, many Mississippians resorted to violence to keep blacks from registering to vote. On June 21, 1964, Congress of Racial Equality (CORE) organizer Michael Schwerner, his assistant James Chaney (a black CORE activist) and Andrew Goodman (a summer volunteer) were arrested by county sheriff and Klan member Cecil Price. Released from jail to a waiting Ku Klux Klan ambush, the three young men were tortured and killed. Their bodies were discovered on August 4. On the forty-first anniversary of the crime, June 21, 2005, Edgar Ray Killen, then eighty years old, was found guilty of the murders and sentenced to three consecutive twenty-year terms. *Resource: McAdam, Doug.* Freedom Summer. *New York: Oxford Univ. Press, 1988.*

the journalist

Helen Zia: One of the most formidable activists in the Asian American community, Helen Zia, a Princeton graduate, has worked for many newspapers and magazines, including the *New York Times* and the *Washington Post*. A staunch feminist, she was also an early opponent of the Vietnam War. One high-profile case in which she exerted her influence as an Asian American activist involved Vincent Chin, a Japanese man beaten to death in June 1982 after an altercation with two white men in a Detroit bar. A second and more prominent case was that of Wen Ho Lee, the Los Alamos scientist who was wrongly accused of being a nuclear spy for the People's Republic of China. President Bill Clinton issued a public apology to Lee over his mistreatment by the U.S. Government. His story is told in *My Country Versus Me,* a book he coauthored with Helen Zia. *Resource: Moyers, Bill.* Becoming an American: The Chinese Experience. *PBS Documentary, 2003.*

the astronaut

Ellison Onizuka: Ellison Shoji Onizuka, a former Eagle Scout from Kealakekua, Kona, Hawaii, was the first Asian American in space. The father of two daughters, he began his Air Force career in 1970. January 24, 1985, marked his first mission—on the space shuttle *Discovery*. He circled the globe forty-eight times and opened NASA's door to outer space for other minorities to follow. The mission specialist on the ill-fated space shuttle *Challenger*, Onizuka and his six crew members perished on January 28, 1986. The chance of a deadly accident during launch phase was 1 in 438. You will find this quotation from him in all new U.S. passports: "Every generation has the obligation to free men's minds for a look at new worlds . . . to look out from a higher plateau than the last generation." *Resource: http://space.about.com/cs/deceasedastronaut/a/ellison onizuka.htm.*

the long walker

Dennis James Banks: Dennis Banks cofounded the American Indian Movement (AIM) in 1968. Its goal: to preserve the customs of Native peoples and protect their rights (to land, hunting, fishing, wild-rice farming) granted to them by long-standing, but often ignored, treaties. He led protests, sit-ins, and nonviolent takeovers of military bases and towns such as Wounded Knee, South Dakota. Hounded by the FBI and police for his principled stands, this lightning rod in the fight against the daily harassment of Indians earned him an unenviable reputation with authorities. He organized long walks ("Sacred Runs")—one from New York to Los Angeles—to call attention to the injustice against his people. *Resource: Stern, Kenneth S.* Loud Hawk (The United States versus the American Indian Movement). *Norman, OK: University of Oklahoma Press, 1994.*

the crusader

Harvey Milk: A Long Islander by birth, Harvey Milk joined the U.S. Navy during the Korean War. After his military duty, he moved from teaching to selling insurance to research on Wall Street, and eventually found himself in San Francisco, where he became increasingly enmeshed in local politics. A firebrand speaker, Milk campaigned openly for gay rights, the issue that defined his life. He eventually became a city councilman and the self-proclaimed "Mayor of Castro Street," an area of the city now, as then, predominantly gay. On November 27, 1978, Dan White, another city councilman, assassinated Milk and his colleague George Moscone, the mayor of San Francisco, because of White's rage at being removed from office and his feeling victimized for his strongly held views against homosexuality. *Resource: Shilts, Randy.* The Mayor of Castro Street: The Life and Times of Harvey Milk. *New York: St. Martin's Press, 1982.*

banker to the poor

Muhammad Yunus: Professor Yunus was born to a Muslim family in what is now Bangladesh, one of the world's poorest nations, where he developed microcredit, an idea that originated with Dr. Akhtar Hameed Khan. Yunus started lending money to the poor—small amounts by bank standards, but an unparalleled opportunity to the country's poorest people, who would not otherwise be able to secure traditional bank loans. He established the Grameen Bank ("Bank of the Villages") to foster economic development "from below." So successful is the bank that it now has over 2,600 branches in 85,000 villages, and has spread to more than 25 other countries. Ninety-seven percent of the eight million borrowers are women, nearly ninety-eight percent of whom have paid back the loans. For his efforts, Professor Yunus and his bank won the Nobel Peace Prize in 2006. *Resource: Bornstein, David.* The Price of a Dream: The Story of the Grameen Bank and the Idea That Is Helping the Poor to Change Their Lives. *New York: Simon & Schuster, 1996.*

the statesman

Nelson Mandela: Once the world's most famous prisoner, Nelson Mandela survived nearly three decades in prison from 1964 to 1990, having been convicted of treason by a white majority intent on keeping organizations like Mandela's, the African National Congress, marginalized, and therefore unable to influence the country's future. Perhaps the most telling aspect of his character during those dreadful years was that he refused to be a victim. In 1994, he was elected to the presidency of South Africa and had to contend with a number of internal crises, but through it all, he maintained his integrity and his undisputed stature in the world. *Resource: Sampson, Anthony.* Mandela: The Authorized Biography. *New York: Vintage Books, 1999.*

the first

Jackie Robinson: It is difficult to exaggerate the importance of Jack Roosevelt Robinson to the game of baseball or to society at large. When he signed with the Brooklyn Dodgers in 1947, he broke the "color bar" by becoming the first black American to play in the major leagues after nearly sixty years of segregation. He then went on to break many records on and off the field in a scintillating career. He was inducted into the Baseball Hall of Fame in 1962. He continued to accomplish historic African American firsts: He was the first television analyst; the first vice president of a major corporation; and one of the founders of the Freedom National Bank in Harlem. His posthumous awards include the Congressional Gold Medal and the Presidential Medal of Freedom. *Resource: Rampersad, Arnold.* Jackie Robinson: A Biography. *New York: Knopf, 1997.*

the child

Sylvia Mendez: The famous 1954 *Brown v. Board of Education* civil rights case declared state laws establishing separate public schools for black and white students unconstitutional. But what preceded *Brown* was *Mendez v. Westminster,* another no-less-important landmark desegregation case. In California in 1946, Hispanics were restricted to "Mexican schools." When Sylvia Mendez and her brothers were barred from a school for "whites only," their parents filed a suit to end separate education. The city of Westminster claimed that facility with English was the critical issue, but their case fell apart when eloquently bilingual Sylvia testified. The court ruled in the Mendez's favor, thereby paving the way for *Brown.* Sylvia continues to tell her story of the great contributions to equal rights that her parents and co-plaintiffs made. *Resource: Meier, Matt S., and Margo Gutierrez.* Encyclopedia of the Mexican American Civil Rights Movement. *Santa Barbara, CA: Greenwood Press, 2000.*